I Know Someone with Asthma

Vic Parker

www.raintreepublishers.co.uk
Visit our website to find out
more information about
Raintree books.

To order:
☎ Phone 0845 6044371
▤ Fax +44 (0) 1865 312263
▥ Email myorders@raintreepublishers.co.uk

Customers from outside the UK please telephone +44 1865 312262

Raintree is an imprint of Capstone Global Library
Limited, a company incorporated in England and
Wales having its registered office at 7 Pilgrim Street,
London, EC4V 6LB – Registered company number:
6695582

Text © Capstone Global Library Limited 2011
First published in hardback in 2011
The moral rights of the proprietor have been asserted.

Edited by Rebecca Rissman, Daniel Nunn
 and Siân Smith
Designed by Joanna Hinton Malivoire
Picture research by Mica Brancic
Originated by Capstone Global Library
Printed and bound in China by Leo Paper Products Ltd

ISBN 978 1 406 22073 5
15 14 13 12 11
10 9 8 7 6 5 4 3 2 1

British Library Cataloguing in Publication Data
Parker, Victoria.
I know someone with asthma. – (Understanding health
issues)
 1. Asthma–Juvenile literature.
 I. Title II. Series
616.2'38-dc22

Acknowledgements
We would like to thank the following for permission
to reproduce photographs: AP/Press Association
Photos p. 20 (LM Otero); Corbis pp. 14 (© JLP/Jose L.
Pelaez), 24 (Icon SMI/© Dustin Snipes); Getty Images
pp. 10 (Michael Zagaris), 22 (Science Photo Library/
Ian Hooton), 25 (Getty Images for British Gas);
iStockphoto.com pp. 5 (© Marilyn Nieves), 9 (© George
M Muresan), 17 (© RMAX), 18 (© Chad Thomas);
Photolibrary p. 16 (Creatas); Science Photo Library pp.
4 (J. Lama, Publiphoto Diffusion), 7 (Peter Gardiner),
13 (Coneyl Jay), 21 (RVI, Newcastle-Upon-Tyne/
Simon Fraser); Shutterstock pp. 11 (© Paul Prescott),
12 (Monkey Business Images), 19 (© Ken Inness), 26
(Jeanne Hatch), 27 (Monkey Business Images (Mandy
Godbehear).

Cover photograph of a girl using an inhaler to treat an
asthma attack reproduced with permission of Science
Photo Library (Ian Hooton).

We would like to thank Matthew Siegel and Ashley
Wolinski for their invaluable help in the preparation of
this book.

Contents

Some words are printed in bold, **like this**. You can
find out what they mean in the glossary.

Do you know someone with asthma?

You might have a friend with asthma. Asthma is a **medical condition** that affects parts of the chest. People with asthma have problems with their breathing.

Someone with asthma may cough a lot, even when they are well.

People with asthma can be more likely to get wheezy when exercising outdoors than indoors.

You might be able to tell someone has asthma by listening to their breathing. They may often be **wheezy**. They may get out of breath quickly when they exercise.

What is asthma?

When we breathe in, we take in air through our nose and mouth. The air goes down into our lungs through tubes called **airways**.

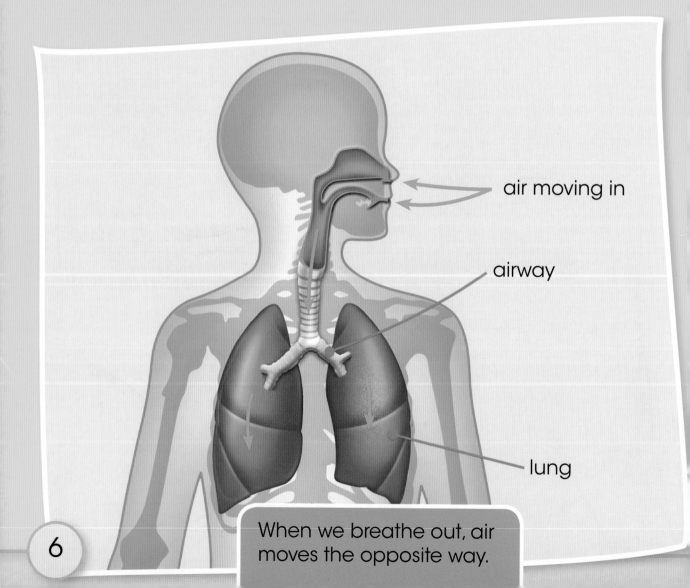

air moving in

airway

lung

When we breathe out, air moves the opposite way.

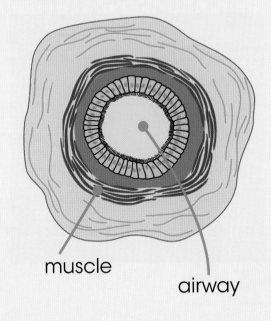

Inside a normal airway

muscle

airway

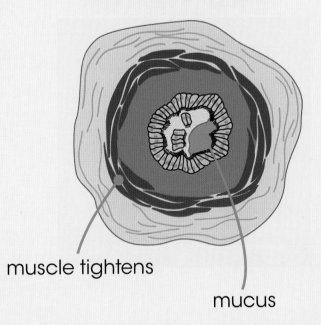

An airway during an asthma attack

muscle tightens

mucus

When a person has asthma, sometimes the inside of their airways becomes swollen and makes gooey stuff called mucus. The muscles around the airways also get tighter. This blocks the airways, making it hard to breathe. This is called an **asthma attack**.

Asthma attacks and triggers

People can have **asthma attacks** when they are around what doctors call '**triggers**'. A trigger is something that can cause an asthma attack or make an attack worse.

Triggers can include:
- cold air
- dust
- furry and feathery animals
- moulds
- some foods
- exercise
- strong smells
- pollution in the air
- strong emotions such as stress.

For some people, cold air is an asthma trigger.

One person's asthma triggers can be different from another's. A person's asthma triggers can also change from time to time.

Everyone is different

Some people need more help with asthma than others.

Some people with asthma find that they are short of breath a lot of the time. They might get **asthma attacks** quite often.

Other people with asthma go for a long time without being affected very much. Then a **trigger** can cause an asthma attack.

When someone knows they will be around things that trigger their asthma, such as feathers, they can take medicine to help control it.

Who gets asthma?

Anyone can get asthma, at any time. However, it can run in families, and people often develop it as children or teenagers. Once you have asthma, you usually have it for life.

It is not possible to catch asthma from someone else.

Tests for asthma include blowing as hard as you can into a spirometer or a peak flow machine. These machines show how well air passes through your **airways**.

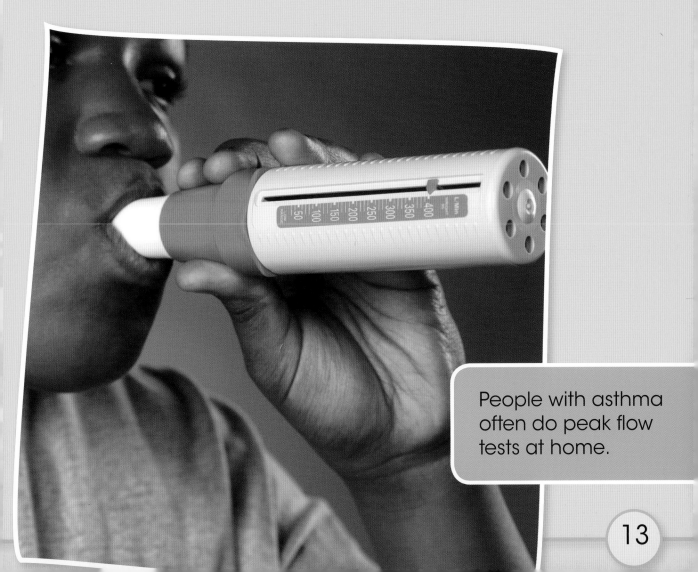

People with asthma often do peak flow tests at home.

Living with asthma

There is currently no **cure** for asthma. However, someone with asthma can lead a full, fun life. It is helpful to keep a diary of **triggers** and **symptoms** or signs of asthma, to discuss with a doctor.

People with asthma can work with their doctor to keep it under control.

People can plan how to avoid their triggers to keep their symptoms as mild as possible. Some things that might help are shown in the table below.

Trigger	Actions
dust	• vacuum often • dust often, with a damp duster • wash soft toys often
animals	• ideally, have no pets • if you have pets, wash them often and don't let them in your bedroom
cold air	• try to play indoors and do indoor sport on cold days
pollen	• don't play outside when the **pollen count** is high

Medicines to control asthma

As well as avoiding **triggers**, many people with asthma need to take medicine every day. This is to control the swelling in their **airways** and stop it from getting worse.

If someone can control their asthma, they can do any sport that someone without asthma can do.

People with asthma each
need to use their own inhaler.

This type of medicine is called controller
medicine. Some controller medicines
are swallowed as tablets or liquids. But
many are breathed in through **inhalers**.

Treatments to relieve asthma

If someone with asthma feels their **symptoms** are getting worse, they can take reliever medicine. This relaxes the muscles around their **airways** and usually works very quickly.

Reliever **inhalers** are also sometimes called 'rescue' inhalers.

Reliever medicine can also help someone with asthma to exercise. If they take it just before exercising, it will keep their airways open. Then they can enjoy their sport.

People with asthma can still become excellent sportspeople.

Emergency!

Occasionally when someone is having an **asthma attack**, taking reliever medicine may not stop the attack from getting worse. Then the person needs to go to hospital straight away.

It is a good idea to call an ambulance if someone needs urgent medical help.

At the hospital, doctors and nurses can give stronger medicines to someone having a severe asthma attack. This usually helps them feel much better.

This equipment can help someone having a severe asthma attack to breathe in strong medicine.

How can you help someone having an asthma attack?

If a friend has a sudden **asthma attack**, it is important to stay calm. They should use their reliever **inhaler** straight away. You should get help from a grown-up.

A person having an asthma attack needs to stay calm and to try to relax.

How you can help:

- you can get your friend their reliever inhaler
- tell a grown-up straight away
- help your friend to stay calm by keeping calm too
- encourage them to sit down instead of lying down or standing up.

Some people can have asthma attacks that are caused by certain foods, such as eggs. These people should always carry a special **injection** with them that can stop the attack for a while.

Famous people

David Beckham has had asthma since he was a child. This has not stopped him from becoming a world-famous footballer.

David Beckham has been given the honour of playing as team captain many times.

Rebecca Adlington has to run and do gym work as well as swim as part of her training.

Chlorine is used in swimming pools to keep water clean. Chlorine can be another asthma **trigger**. But Rebecca Adlington is a British swimmer with asthma who has won two Olympic gold medals!

Being a good friend

You can be a good friend to someone with asthma by finding out what **triggers** their asthma. Try to do things together that keep you away from their asthma triggers.

Good friends understand each other.

We all have different bodies and personalities.

Living with asthma can be difficult at times. We are all different in many ways. A good friend likes us and values us for who we are.

Asthma – facts and fiction

Facts

- About 300 million people in the world have asthma.

- More boys have asthma than girls.

- Colds and the flu can make asthma worse.

Fiction

(?) People with asthma are short of breath all the time.

WRONG! Some have **symptoms** only occasionally.

(?) People with asthma can't exercise.

WRONG! Someone with controlled asthma can do any exercise.

(?) You aren't more likely to get asthma if your parents smoke.

WRONG! Children whose parents smoke are 1½ times more likely to develop asthma.

Glossary

airway tube in your body that air travels through to get to your lungs

asthma attack when someone has difficulty breathing due to asthma

cure medical treatment that makes someone better

inhaler people use an inhaler to take medicine into their bodies by breathing it in

injection people use an injection to take medicine into their bodies through a needle

medical condition health problem that a person has for a long time or for life

pollen count measurement of the amount of pollen in the air. Pollen is made by plants.

symptoms signs of an illness

trigger something that can cause an asthma attack or make an attack worse

wheezing to make a high, rough noise due to difficulties breathing

Find out more

Books to read

Asthma (It's not catching), Angela Royston (Heinemann Library, 2004)

Feeling Ill: Asthma, Jillian Powell (Evans Brothers, 2007)

I have asthma (Let's Talk About It), Jennifer Moore-Mallinos (Barron's Educational Series Inc USA, 2007)

Websites

kidshealth.org/kid/centers/asthma_center. html
Watch an animation that shows what happens during an asthma attack on this website.

www.kickasthma.org.uk
Asthma UK's website for children and young people with asthma has a mix of information, games, and interactive sections.

Index